ANSWERS
TO MY
CATHOLIC
FRIENDS

THOMAS F. HEINZE

CHICK
PUBLICATIONS

PO Box 662, Chino, CA 91708-0662 USA

—————— INTERNATIONAL DISTRIBUTORS ——————

Christ The Way Publications, Inc.
P.O. Box 43120, Eastwood Square
Kitchener, Ont. N5H 6S9, Canada

B. McCall Barbour
28 George IV Bridge
Edinburgh, Scotland/UK EH1 1ES
Tel: 0131-225 4816

New Zealand Evangelistic Society
P.O. Box 50096
Porirua, Wellington, New Zealand

Evangelistic Literature Enterprise
P.O. Box 5010
Brendale, Q'ld., Australia 4500
Tel: (07) 3205-7100

Gospel Publishers
P.O. Box 1
Westhoven 2142, South Africa
Tel: (11) 673-3157
Fax: (11) 673-2644

Sword Distributors
P.O. Box 3459
Parklands 2121, South Africa
Tel/Fax: (011) 486-3361

Chick Gospel Literatur
Postfach 1166
D-51387 Burscheid
Germany
Tel. 02174/63815
Fax: 02174/2799

CHICK PUBLICATIONS
P. O. Box 662, Chino, CA 91708-0662 USA
Tel: (909) 987-0771 • Fax: (909) 941-8128
World Wide Web: www.chick.com
E Mail: postmaster@chick.com

Printed in the United States of America

ISBN: 0-937958-52-2
Library of Congress Card Catalog Number: 96-083168

Contents

Preface

As an evangelical missionary in Italy for over thirty years, I have found that there are certain things that Roman Catholics would like to know about the faith of the Protestants and about the Bible. Moreover, they want clear, unevasive answers. The ecumenical movement in their own church has made it more important than ever for them to have this information. If you are a Roman Catholic, read on. You will find some of the answers surprising. You will want to take your own Bible and check them for yourself from God's word. As you do, if you will start reading several verses before those that I refer to, and then read several verses after as well, it will help you understand the context so you can see for yourself that I am using them honestly. You will also get more out of the Bible itself, and the study will be a benefit to your spiritual life as well as providing information you really wanted to know.

The Bible passages which are quoted in this booklet are not taken from any Protestant edition of the Bible, but from the Roman Catholic Bible, *The New American Bible,* translated by members of the Catholic Biblical Association of America and fully approved by the Roman Catholic Church.

1

Do You Have The Mass Like
The Catholic Church?

This is a very important question, since the mass is the heart of most Roman Catholic meetings. Protestants have the Lord's supper, also called the communion, which, though it resembles the mass, is not the same. The outward form of the mass has been modified to make it much more similar to our communion service than it was when it was said in Latin, but the differences in its basic meaning remain.

The Roman Catholic doctrine of the mass was established at the Council of Trent, which affirmed, among other things, that it is, "a sacrifice of expiation... of sins and the punishment for sins... not merely for the living, but also for the poor souls in Purgatory" (Ludwig Ott, Fundamentals of Catholic Dogma, pp. 412-413). The Roman church thus teaches that Christ's sacrifice is renewed in the mass, and that each time the mass is said, this renewing of His sacrifice adds a bit of merit that can count toward one's salvation. When the mass is said for the dead, it is supposed to reduce by an unknown amount, the time they must suffer in purgatory for their sins.

In practice, many people, probably the majority in most Roman Catholic countries, have been taught that after a death in the family, they must give more or less unending offerings to the priests for masses to shorten their loved one's time in purgatory. This is particularly tragic for the widows who are often poor and very religious. While many priests are not in agreement with this doctrine, and do not even accept offerings for the mass in these conditions, others bring to one's mind the admonition of Christ in the Scriptures, *Be on guard against the scribes, who like to parade around in their robes and accept marks of respect in public, front seats in the synagogues, and places of honor at banquets. These men devour the savings of widows and recite long prayers for appearance' sake; it is they who will receive the severest sentence* (Mark 12:38-40) In Italy, the very heart of Roman Catholicism, there is a saying which is often used when someone wants to say "you only get what you pay for." Translated word for word it is, "Without money, they don't sing the mass."

Do the Bread and Wine Become Christ's Body And Blood?

As a foundation for the teaching that Christ's sacrifice can and should be renewed in the mass, Roman Catholic doctrine insists that the bread and wine used in the communion service are changed by a miracle. This miracle is not evident, that is, the substances still look like bread and wine. Nevertheless, Catholic doctrine insists that they actually become the flesh and blood of Jesus, and are no longer bread and wine. This supposed miracle is called transubstantiation. It is based on a tradition which started to enter the church around 300 AD., but did not become a dogma until the year 1215 A.D. It was after this, around the year 1226, that Catholics began to bow down before the bread. The church, having accepted this tradition, tries to give the practice the appearance of a biblical basis with a strange interpretation of these words of Jesus Christ: *...and after He had given thanks, broke it and said, "This is my body, which is for you. Do this in remembrance of me." In the same way, after the supper, He took the cup, saying, "This cup is the new covenant in my blood. Do this, whenever you drink it, in remembrance of me. ...this cup is the new covenant in my blood"* (1 Corinthians 11:24-25). The Catholic interpretation is that the bread and wine which Christ held in His hand was by a miracle transformed into His body.

Some try to reduce this to simply a question of literal or figurative interpretation of this scripture. However, it is more. Please note that when Christ said these words He was standing before His disciples in His body, holding up the bread and wine so that it was clear that the words *This is my body* were intended to be understood symbolically. There can be no doubt of this because after He stated, *This is my body,* He called it bread three times, which He certainly would not have done if at that point it was no longer bread, but had literally become His body *(every time you eat this bread...* 1 Corinthians 11:26-28). Since Christ called the substance both *bread,* and *body,* He must have been speaking symbolically either when He called it bread, or when He called it body. The question is not,

"Should we interpret the passage literally or symbolical-ly?" The question is "Which part must be interpreted liter-ally and which part symbolically?" Was Christ speaking literally when he called the substance which He held in His hand his body, or when he called it bread? One or the other must have been symbolic. The only other choice is that it changed from bread to body, then back to bread.

We find a similar statement in Mark 14:25, when Jesus calls the wine, *fruit of the vine,* after the point at which, according to Catholic doctrine, it should no longer have been fruit of the vine, but should have been completely transformed into the blood of Christ. If it had already been literally changed into blood, would Jesus not have called it *blood* instead of *fruit of the vine?* He also said, *I am the door.* Did He not mean that it is through Him that we can enter heaven, rather than that the substance of his body had been changed into wood?

Even more important is the fact that in the mass, at the moment that the miracle should occur, nothing happens! By way of comparison, Christ also changed water into wine. In this case, it was clear to all that it was no longer water, but had actually become wine: *The waiter in charge tasted the water made wine, without knowing where it came from; only the other waiters knew, since they had drawn the water. Then the waiter in charge called the groom over and remarked to him: "People usually serve the choice wine first; then when the guests have been drinking awhile, a lesser vintage. What you have done is keep the choice wine until now"* (John 2:8-10). Think of Christ's other miracles. When He healed the paralytic and the man who was lame, did they continue to lie there as if nothing had happened?

Let us not lose sight of the true purpose of the communion service. Christ never once told His disciples to offer his body again, but He told them twice, to partake *in remembrance of Him* (1 Corinthians 11:24-25). We honor Christ by doing what He commands.

Can Christ's Sacrifice Be Renewed?

With these Scriptures as a background, we are ready to examine the strong evidence of Hebrews chapter 10, verses 10-18. I encourage you to study the chapters before this as well, not only to see that I am not taking verses out of context to change the meaning, but because chapters seven and nine also discuss this subject.

Hebrews 10:10 tells us bluntly that the sacrifice of Christ can not be renewed. ...*We have been sanctified through the offering of the body of Jesus Christ once for all* (See also Romans 6:9-10). It is clear from this verse that there is no necessity or possibility of further sacrifice because it says that Christ's body was offered once for all. The passage, however, does not stop here but goes on to state with even more detail and clarity, *Every other priest stands ministering day by day and offering again and again those same sacrifices which can never take away sins. But Jesus offered one sacrifice for sins and took his seat forever at the right hand of God* (Hebrews 10:11-12). Here Jesus is contrasted with the Hebrew priests who offer repeated sacrifices. What is the difference between them and Jesus? Jesus does not stand *offering again and again those same sacrifices,* but he has offered one sacrifice which was enough. As He died on the cross he stated, "It is finished." How does the daily renewal of his sacrifice in the mass fit with these verses? It does not! It contradicts them. It is exactly the opposite.

The last part of this passage gives a reason why Christ's sacrifice can not be renewed. *He took his seat forever at the right hand of God.* This is in complete agreement with the Bible's explanation that as His disciples watched, Christ, *was lifted up before their eyes in a cloud which took Him from their sight* (Acts 1:9). Where is Christ now? He went up to heaven, where, as this passage states, He *took his seat forever at the right hand of God. Forever* means that He is still there (See Acts 3:21).

Many think that Christ's body is in the consecrated wafer in the tabernacle at the front of every Roman Catholic Church, and they bow to it whenever they pass. If this were true, perhaps his sacrifice could be renewed, but the Scripture clearly states that He offered one single sacrifice which was adequate for our complete salvation, and that His body is now in heaven. We are to take the bread and wine *in remembrance of* Him (1 Corinthians 11:24-25).

One of the things we remember is His one sufficient sacrifice. Bowing before the bread is idolatry because it is bread and not Jesus Christ. In addition, if we become confused and think that the wafer is Christ, we are apt to lose the significance of communion, and miss taking it in remembrance of Him.

The Catholic doctrine of the repeated renewal of Christ's

sacrifice keeps many from heaven because it infers that Christ's sacrifice on the cross for our sins was insufficient. If not, why would it need to be repeated many times?

The idea that Christ's sacrifice was not enough is then used to lead us to believe that the person who dies must suffer in purgatory to pay for his own sins until Christ has been offered enough times to work up the merit necessary to finish off the payment. Our passage in Hebrews 10 leaves no doubt about this, however. It goes on in verse 14 to say, *By one offering he has forever perfected those who are being sanctified.* Let us put our trust in Christ, and His ability to perfect us by *one offering,* instead of denying His salvation by considering His sacrifice insufficient.

A few lines down, in Hebrews 10:17 and 18, another important promise is added, *Their sins and their transgressions I will remember no more. Once these have been forgiven, there is no further offering for sin.* Christ's sacrifice took care of our sins so completely that God is able to forgive them and to forget them. Where is Purgatory then? It is certainly not taught in the Bible! It teaches instead that when we trust our salvation to Jesus Christ who paid for them with one sacrifice, God forgives and forgets our sins. Those who try to get to heaven in some other way go to hell. The Bible knows no middle ground.

This wonderful truth calls for action! Why don't you pause for a moment, and thank God that Christ's one sacrifice was enough. Trust Him to save you, and believe His promise that God really will forgive you and forget all about your sins. *Once these have been forgiven, there is no further offering for sin.*

2

Where Do The Differences Between Catholics And Protestants Come From?

Many people tell me, "You Protestants interpret the Bible one way, and the Catholic church another!" The differences, however, are for the most part not really differences of interpretation, but of authority. For Biblical Protestants, the authority is the Word of God. A priest summed this up very well when he exclaimed to me with disgust, "You Protestants believe everything that book says!"

The Biblical emphasis which is the heritage of the Protestant churches is visible even in the architecture of its buildings. In the Catholic church the altar is central. There the sacrifice of Christ is believed to be renewed in the mass. In the Protestant churches the pulpit is the center of attention. It is essentially a stand to hold the Bible in a position where it is easy for the preacher to read because the reading and explanation of the word of God is central.

The Catholic church does officially accept the Bible as the inspired Word of God, but not as the final authority. Tradition, along with the pronouncements of Popes and

Councils is considered equally authoritative. There are, however, many points in which the tradition of the Catholic church is not in agreement with the Bible. It is at these points that each one of us must decide which he will follow.

A Changing Church

In deciding whether to submit to the authority of the Bible or that of the Church, we need to take into consideration the fact that what the Catholic Church believes to be right or wrong changes with the passing of time. To have the communion service in the language of the people was, at one time, a Protestant heresy. The mass had to be said in Latin. Then came a period of reform started by Pope John the twenty third, when it had to be in the languages of the people instead. The Bible, however, does not change and therefore cannot always agree with a changing church.

An elderly Catholic lady once told me, "If the Pope wants to eat meat on Fridays and go to hell, he can, but I'm not going to!" Since the Bible agrees with the present Catholic doctrine that eating meat on Fridays is not sin, it could not agree earlier that eating meat on Fridays was sin.

Down through the centuries, many changes have also entered into the church's teaching which are strongly in disagreement with the Bible. We might illustrate this with the acceptance of the veneration of images in the church. (See chapter four). Differences between Catholic doctrine, and that of those for whom the Bible is the final authority do not result from a Protestant desire to be obnoxious, but rather from the fact that where there is a conflict between the teachings of the Bible and those of the Catholic church, it is impossible to accept both. Each person must choose in these points which authority he will obey.

For the most part, the traditions that are in contrast with the Bible began to form after 300 A.D. in the time of the Roman emperor Constantine, and gradually developed until they became dogmas of the Church, though a few of the anti-biblical doctrines are very recent.

Protestant Influence in the Catholic Church

A more recent development, and one which is harder to evaluate is that of the ecumenical movement which, when it first began, was not in the Catholic Church. It started in the liberal (also called modernist) wing of the Protestant churches; that is, among those Protestant churches which no longer really believed the Bible. As a result they no longer held to some of the most fundamental Biblical teachings such as salvation being a gift of God which is received through faith in Jesus Christ. Because of this drift in faith, they no longer had a clear message to offer. The result was that the liberal churches started to diminish in attendance.

Where a large congregation had been easily able to maintain its large church building, a smaller group was now having trouble. Often this was also true of the church of another liberal denomination just around the corner. Why not get together, put both congregations in one of the buildings, sell the other, and solve the economic problems of the diminishing churches? Thus practical financial motivation as well as the desirability of oneness combined to begin the ecumenical movement among the Protestant churches.

Roman Catholicism found itself attracted to the ecumenical ideal of unity, but it had a practical motivation as well, that of offering the Roman Catholic Church as the one fold into which all denominations should come. To prepare a Catholicism into which Protestants might feel more free to enter, Bible reading began to be encouraged among Catholics, and changes were made in the Roman Catholic liturgy to make it more like what Protestants were used to.

Unfortunately, however, in their desire to be like Protestants, many Catholic seminaries began teaching the philosophies of the liberal theologians who had led so many Protestant churches away from the Bible. The results were the same. Roman Catholic church attendance started to diminish too, giving the Roman church the same powerful practical financial motivation for combining churches that the liberal Protestant groups had.

While the influence of the Bible has been increasing among some Catholics because they are reading it more now that the church permits it, other Catholics are being swayed by liberal attacks on the Bible's truthfulness.

Another new development in the Catholic Church which has also come to it from the Protestants is the Charismatic movement which started in a Protestant church in California in 1901. It gave rise first to the Pentecostal churches, and then, spilling across denominational lines, to the Catholic Charismatic movement.

Why Follow the Bible?

Down through the centuries the Bible has been hated and destroyed as no other book. Probably more copies of the Bible have been burned than of all other books put together, yet today more people read it, more people own it, and it is translated into more languages and published in more copies than any other book.

Not only do millions read this book today, but millions of others in the past have given their lives to make its message known. Why?

• Because it has made sinful lives good and worthwhile. Through its influence they have come to know God and to be a help to those around them.

• Because it is inspired of God. *All Scripture is inspired of God...* (2 Timothy 3:16). In addition to saying so, it gives convincing evidence of really being inspired by God; for example many of its prophecies have already been fulfilled. Catholic doctrine also states that this book is inspired of God.

• The Bible contains everything that is necessary to bring the Christian to perfection. The verse quoted above continues, *All Scripture is inspired of God and is useful for teaching - for reproof, correction, and training in holiness so that the man of God may be fully competent and equipped for every good work* (2 Timothy 3:16-17). We need add nothing from tradition to bring the believer to this fully competent and equipped state.

• Because, as the apostle Peter informs us in his second letter, the Bible is more reliable than that which he had seen with his eyes and heard with his ears because it was written by men impelled by the Holy Spirit (1 Peter 1:16-21). It would seem obvious that if the Bible is more reliable than what Peter himself had seen and heard, it is also more reliable than any tradition which contradicts it.

Some misinterpret a part of this Scripture and say that only the Roman Catholic church is capable of interpreting the Bible. The passage, however, speaks of God's guidance of those who wrote the Bible, and does not say that only certain ones can interpret it. The apostle Paul praised the believers of Berea for examining the Scriptures for themselves to see if what he was teaching them was really Scriptural: *Its members were better disposed than those in Thessalonica, and welcomed the message with great enthusiasm. Each day they studied the Scriptures to see whether these things were so* (Acts 17:11). If they did well to test the teachings of the apostle Paul by comparing them with the Scriptures that they already had, how much more should we apply the same test to the traditions of the church today?

The New Testament speaks a great deal about tradition, and condemns it when it is contrary to the word of God. Jesus said: *You disregard God's commandment and cling to what is human tradition... That is the way you nullify God's word in favor of the traditions you have handed on* (Mark 7:8,13; see also Matthew 15:2-6; Colossians 2:8; 1 Thessalonians 2:13; Galatians 1:14).

Some, trying to justify the authority of the Catholic church over that of the Scriptures, remind us that the Bible does not contain everything that Jesus and the apostles taught. This is certainly true and the Bible itself affirms it. This fact, however, gives us no authorization to accept the many Catholic doctrines which are explicitly contrary to teachings of Scripture (Revelations 22:18-19; Mark 7:3-13). The Bible contains all that is needed to bring us to faith in Christ, and to help us grow in that faith. (John 20:30-31; 2 Timothy 3:16-17).

The great majority of the differences between Bible believing Protestants and the Roman Catholic Church do not come from different interpretations of the Bible or different Bibles, but from a difference in what is the "final authority." The Bible must be interpreted in the light of the Bible itself and neither twisted nor set aside to honor the pronouncement of popes, councils, or tradition (2 Thessalonians 2:15; 3:6).

3

What Is The Most Important Difference Between Protestants And Catholics?

If someone came to you today and asked, "How can I be saved? I want to go to heaven and not to hell! What should I do?" what would you tell him?

I have asked this question of thousands of Roman Catholics, and ask it of you. Almost all give substantially the same answer. It is the same answer I as a Protestant gave before my salvation, when I did not yet know the answer God gives in the Bible. This answer could be summarized: "Be good. Don't sin. Live by God's law."

The Great Surprise: We Cannot Merit Salvation

The Bible teaches us the exact opposite of that which most of us have believed! It teaches us that we are sinners who do not merit salvation. *All men have sinned... Not one of them acts uprightly, no, not one* (Romans 3:23, 12). We are all included! The Bible teaches that we are not good enough to save our souls. *Cursed is he who does not abide by everything written in the book of the law to carry it out* (Galatians 3:10). God asks us to abide by *everything*, not simply to be better than others, but *abide by everything!*

Some of us abide by more than others, but no one is perfect. Even though none of us abides by *everything written in the book of the law,* God still loves us, and in His love, He gives us the good news of the Gospel. That is, that in spite of what we deserved, He has had mercy on us, and has sent His son to pay for our sins.

Sometimes a guilty and condemned criminal waiting to be executed is handed a complete pardon from the governor. God did that for us: *The wages of sin is death, but the gift of God is eternal life through Jesus Christ our Lord* (Romans 6:23). Yes, *God so loved the world that He gave his only Son, that whoever believes in Him may not die but may have eternal life* (John 3:16).

God explains that we cannot save ourselves, but that salvation is His gift to us sinners: *I repeat, it is owing to His favor that salvation is yours through faith. This is not your doing, it is God's gift; neither is it a reward for anything you have accomplished, so let no one pride himself on it* (Ephesians 2:8-9).

Notice how the Bible completely contradicts the fond belief of so many people that if they try hard enough they will be able to save themselves by keeping God's law: *Never-the-less, knowing that a man is not justified by legal observance but by faith in Jesus Christ, we too have believed in Him in order to be justified by faith in Christ, not by observance of the law; for by works of the law no one will be justified* (Galatians 2:16). And again, *the just man shall live by faith* (Galatians 3:10-11). (See also Galatians 3:12-13; 5:4; Romans 3:20).

The criminal who is handed a pardon, does not receive it because he is better than other criminals. He is guilty and condemned. But he had faith that that piece of paper would really free him. He gave it a try and walked out a free man. In Jesus Christ, God offers His pardon to undeserving sinners. What will you do with it?

Christ's Death Was Not a Stupid Mistake

The Bible says that if it were possible for us to merit salvation by keeping God's law, there would have been no reason for Christ to die for us. *I will not treat God's gracious gift as pointless. If justice is available through the law, then Christ died to no purpose!* (Galatians 2:21).

The Bible explains both why we cannot merit our salvation, and what Christ did about it. He died in our place, and took upon Himself our punishment. *All men have sinned, and are deprived of the glory of God. All men are now undeservedly justified by the gift of God, through the redemption wrought in Christ Jesus. Through His blood, God made Him the means of expiation for all who believe... so that He might be just and might justify those who believe in Jesus... For we hold that a man is justified by faith apart from observance of the law* (Romans 3:23-28). This passage also explains who will be justified: *those who believe in Jesus.*

God says, *All men have sinned.* Take His word for it. Don't try to convince Him that you are an exception. Repent of your sins because Christ died on the cross to pay the penalty for them, not just for the original sin of Adam, but for all sins. The Apostle John wrote, ...*the blood of His Son Jesus cleanses us from all sin* (1 John 1:7). Accept the pardon He offers you!

The Other Way Won't Work

In Italy, when a pope dies, great posters are plastered on the walls of the cities calling the people to pray for his soul because the church believes that he is suffering in purgatory. Roman Catholicism, very frankly, cannot save even its own popes. If you are trusting in that system for your salvation, you should fervently hope for one of two things:

• That the Bible is wrong about how one is saved.

• That you are a better Catholic than the popes.

Let's face the truth: The Bible is not wrong, and you probably are not a better Catholic than the popes. The wonderfully good news is that God offers salvation in His Son for sinners that have not earned it.

Please Receive God's Gift

Salvation, as we read earlier, is God's gift to us. All we must do to receive a gift is to accept it (Ephesians 2:8-9). To accept God's gift of salvation means to accept His Son because, *God gave us eternal life, and this life is in His Son. Whoever possesses the Son possesses life; whoever does not possess the Son of God does not possess life...* (1 John 5:11-12).

For you to accept Christ means to stop believing that you can save yourself by your baptism, by being good enough or by your own suffering in purgatory. Shift your faith to a more solid foundation. Trust Christ to save you!

Ask Him to enter your life and to cleanse it as He wishes. When you do, God no longer sees you in your sin, but in Christ's goodness. John, the apostle that Jesus loved most, wrote, *All who did accept Him, He empowered to become children of God* (John 1:12). The apostle Paul experienced this in his own life, and wrote, *Now that we have been justified by faith, we are at peace with God through our Lord Jesus Christ. Through Him we have gained access by faith to the grace in which we now stand...* (Romans 5:1-2).

In my own experience, when I realized that God was asking me to trust Christ to save me, I had a real struggle. He was asking me to give up what I had always counted on for my salvation; my own goodness and merit. An artist captured this thought with a picture of a child who was dropping a toy to make room for a beautiful bird that was flying down to land on her hand.

I was not what I considered a very bad sinner when I first understood that God was offering me salvation in Christ. As I considered my life, the one outstanding thing that bothered me was that I used a filthy vocabulary that I knew God was not pleased with. I felt that if I could only clean this up, I would be worthy of my salvation.

I had another motivation for cleaning up this sin as well. I was a university student at the time, and wanted very much to make a good impression on the girls, but I was often very embarrassed to find my habitual dirty language popping out at the most inappropriate moments.

At one point, I even enlisted the help of a friend. Every time he heard me say a dirty word, I paid a fine. In a very short time he had accumulated a good sum of money

which we spent for an evening out on the town. But nothing worked! I couldn't control the only sin I can think of
which offers the sinner nothing. Had I been a thief, I
would have had more money. Sexual sin would have given
me an occasional moment of pleasure. But despite the fact
that my filthy language offered me nothing in return, I still
couldn't kick the habit. Seeing this, I abandoned every
hope of ever being good enough to save myself, and
believed God. It was a humbling moment and a very diffi-
cult decision. I faced the fact that I had been wrong for 18
years and asked Christ to come into my heart and cleanse
me.

The tears of relief at the end of this inner struggle were
still running down my cheeks as I walked off a new man,
saved by grace, not by works, and bound for heaven.
Christ living in me soon cleaned up my vocabulary, and
has been cleaning things up ever since.

I have seen the same thing happen to all kinds of sinners
since then, from the most righteous of sinners, to thieves
on drugs who stole the last dollar their own mother had to
buy groceries. Letting Christ cleanse a life after He saves a
soul is not always easy. It takes time reading His word to
let Him persuade us, but God sends the Spirit of Christ to
live in us when we receive His Son, and we are cleansed
by His power and not our own. That is the secret.

You too can be saved today by a simple sincere act of
faith. Jesus said, *All that the Father gives me shall come to
me; no one who comes will I ever reject* (John 6:37). Will
you pause and come to Jesus right now to get this thing
settled? You will not be rejected! If you need to, read

again anything you have not understood, but don't put off your decision. Nothing else that you may do with your life will be of much importance if you go to hell, so why not confess your sins to God Himself right now. As you do, believe that Christ paid for every one of those sins.

Next I would suggest that you thank Him. Show Him that you mean it, by spending time in His Word, the Bible, every day to have fellowship with Him, and find out what He really wants from your life. Christ is your Lord and master, as well as your Savior. He wants to guide in what you do with your life.

Ask God, and He will help you to find fellowship with other Christians in a group that really believes and follows His word. He will also help you bring your friends to Him.

4

Why Don't Protestants Venerate Images?

To those who live in the fringe areas of Roman Catholicism the problem of images does not seem as important as it actually is. At its center in Italy the attitude toward images is still the criteria which most Catholics use to distinguish between Catholics and Protestants. They will say, "Oh! You're an Evangelical! You're the ones who don't believe in the saints, aren't you?"

Catholic dogma states, "It is permissible and profitable to venerate images of the Saints." These images, and the saints which they represent, are extremely important to the religious life of the people of Italy and of other strongly Roman Catholic countries. This is not only true in the church itself, but it is also true of the less official folk religion. Multitudes who almost never darken the door of a church consider themselves devoted Catholics simply because they are devoted to one or more Catholic images.

Perhaps the one most important fact which distinguishes Bible believing Protestants from their Catholic neighbors is the Protestant insistence that each individual needs to know God personally. In fact, the very reason that Christ came to earth, died for our sins, and rose again was to take away the sins that separate us from God, so that we can know Him in a personal way. The Bible teaches that each individual should have a continual relationship directly with God; not a long distance relationship through an image or the saint that the image represents. One of the major themes in the Bible, from its beginning in Genesis, all the way through to the last book, Revelation, is the Lord's hatred for images. The reason is that they separate man from direct contact with Him by providing something else to pray to and trust in.

Mystery of the Missing Commandment

Most Catholics are very surprised to find that one of the ten commandments prohibits the use of images. I quote the second commandment, not from some Protestant publication, but from the Roman Catholic Bible. *You shall not carve idols for yourselves in the shape of anything in the sky above or on the earth below or in the waters beneath the earth; you shall not bow down before them or worship them. For I, the Lord, your God, am a jealous God, inflicting punishment for their fathers' wickedness on the children of those who hate me, down to the third and fourth generation; but bestowing mercy down to the thousandth generation, on the children of those who love me and keep my commandments.* (Exodus 20:4-6).

While the Catholic Church regularly teaches the Ten Commandments in its catechisms, it consistently eliminates the commandment quoted above. Nevertheless, it is always found in whatever Bible, whether printed by a Catholic or Protestant printing press. If you have a Bible, why don't you look it up right now?

If you have a Roman Catholic Catechism, why don't you open it up, too. You will not immediately notice that the commandment against making images and bowing before them has been eliminated, because there will still be ten commandments, but if you will read the first three commandments in both the Bible and the Catechism, you will notice that the second commandment, the longest of all, has been left out in the version found in the Catechism. The omission has been hidden by splitting the tenth commandment into two. Here is how the tenth commandment reads in the Catholic Bible: *Thou shall not covet your neighbor's house. You shall not covet your neighbor's wife, nor his male or female servant, nor his ox or ass, nor anything else that belongs to him.* (Exodus 20:17). In the Catechism, the part about not coveting your neighbor's wife becomes the ninth, and the rest, servant, etc. are grouped together to form the tenth. These commandments are repeated again in Deuteronomy 5. In this second passage it is not as noticeable that the last commandment has been split in two to camouflage the theft of the second. This is probably why the Catholic church normally uses the review of the Ten Commandments in Deuteronomy instead of the original giving of the commandments in Exodus.

The fact that the second commandment is skipped altogether and the omission hidden shows that it is not a matter of the Catholic Church interpreting it differently from the way others do. If they did not understand that it condemns their images why would they have removed this commandment from the catechism and from other popular Catholic teaching?

Photographs

Some, in an attempt to justify praying to images, say that if we had to literally observe the second commandment, we could not even have photographs of our friends and loved ones. The Bible clarifies this point in a passage which specifies what images it is condemning. The prohibited images are those that people venerate or worship: *Do not make false gods for yourselves. You shall not erect an idol or a sacred pillar for yourselves, nor shall you set up a stone figure for worship in your land; for I, the Lord, am your God* (Leviticus 26:1). Notice that here, as in Exodus, it speaks of a purpose for using the image, *for worship,* the same Hebrew word is often translated "to bow down." This purpose would not exclude normal photographs of your friends and family. An obvious exception is the practice of praying to photos of dead relatives.

Pagan Images

Others try to avoid God's clear teaching by stating in an authoritative way that He is only referring to pagan images and not their "Christian" images. However, we notice that:

• Moses, speaking to the Hebrews, God's chosen people and not to pagans, told them that the Lord had not shown Himself to them when He gave them the ten commandments for a precise reason: So that God's people would not make images of God Himself, *You saw no form at all on the day the Lord spoke to you at Horeb from the midst of the fire. Be strictly on your guard, therefore, not to degrade yourselves by fashioning an idol to represent any figure, whether it be the form of a man or a woman...* (Deuteronomy 4:15-16, read also verses 17-29). What was prohibited here was not a pagan image, but any images that God's chosen people might have made of God Himself or of men or women.

• God praised a king of the Jews for destroying a brass serpent which had previously been made at His express commandment and which His people, after a certain period of time, had begun to venerate. The Bible says of this king, *He pleased the Lord, just as his forefather David had done. It was he who removed the high places, shattered the pillars, and cut down the sacred poles. He smashed the bronze serpent called Nehushten which Moses had made, because up to that time the Israelites were burning incense to it* (2 Kings 18:3-4).

Images Are Prohibited in the New Testament

Others, in trying to escape the clear teaching of God's word, claim that images were prohibited in the Old Testament, but are now allowed since we are no longer in the times of the Old Testament, but of the New. The fatal weakness of this argument is that it is just not true! The New Testament speaks a great deal about images, and always against them, just as does the Old Testament.

One of the earlier passages to be written in the New Testament is 1 Corinthians 10:14, *I am telling you, whom I love, to shun the worship of idols.* This theme runs right

through the New Testament. We even find it in 1 John
5:21, one of the last books to be written in the New
Testament. There we read, *My little children, be on your
guard against idols.*

In between these verses which I have quoted are others,
too numerous to list here, but I encourage you to look
them up for yourself. You will see that images are prohibited more or less all through the New Testament: 1
Corinthians 6:9, 10:7; 12:2; Acts 7:39-42, 17:16, 29;
Romans 1:23; 1 Peter 4:3; Rev. 2:14, 9:20, 21:8, 22:15.

History of Idolatry in the Church

The churches of the first centuries did not use images
(with the exception of the symbol of the fish, used like a
logo and not an idol). Images first entered the church for
ornamental use around the end of the third century. By 400
A.D. they were also being used for instructional purposes,
and only in the centuries following were these images
regarded as sacred. They were then accepted for veneration by the Roman Church in the council of Nicea in 787
A.D. and in that of Trent in 1562 A.D.

According to Catholic tradition, when a person prays to
or worships the image of a saint, he is venerating the saint
himself. This explanation, however convincing it may
sound, can never justify praying to an image, because God
commands us not to. This fact has been understood by
some of the most important people in the Catholic church.
Under the reform started by Pope John the twenty-third,
many of the images were taken out of the churches. Pope
John, and several other popes who followed him, also tried

to cut down on other idolatrous practices of the church, such as carrying images in processions.

Whose Images?

In the majority of cases, the images that are venerated are not really images of the saints, as there were no cameras during the lives of most of them and not many of them posed for painted pictures. The obvious consequence is that frequently the images actually are those of models that later artists hired. Many artists created both religious and non-religious art and used the same models for both. Sometimes the artist's models were very religious people, but often they were not. On other occasions the mental pictures in the mind of the artists determined how the saint would look. This becomes obvious as one recalls the pale complexion common to many of the "Madonnas," and then remembers the famous black "Madonnas."

One lady learned that what people are praying to are often not really images of the saints. While walking her dog, she passed by the door of an artist's studio. The artist stepped out and stopped her to ask if he might clip a bit of hair from her dogs' tail for the eyebrows of a saint he was making. She willingly gave him the hair he wanted. Then as she walked away, she realized, "This means that I am going to be bowing down to the hair of my dog's tail!" She put a stop to her own idolatry then and there.

Images Are One of the Major Subjects of the Bible

The fact that so many passages of the Bible deal with images makes it quite obvious that in God's estimation, this is an extremely important issue. I have already pointed out many of the passages in the New Testament. While the subject is too vast in the Old Testament to list all of the passages, the following are among the most important, and reading them will make God's view of images very clear. In addition, their sheer numbers cannot help but impress us with the importance of this subject in God's sight: Exodus 23:24, 34:13; Leviticus 19:4, 26:30; Numbers 33:52; Deuteronomy 5:8-9, 9:12-17, 16:21, 27:15; 1 Kings 14:9, 22-23; Psalms 78:58, 97:7, 106:19-20, **115:4-9,** 135:15-18; Isaiah 10:10-11, 30:22, 31:6-7, 42:8-17, **44:8-20,** 45:20, **46:6-7; Jeremiah 10:3-16,** Ezekiel 16:17-21, 30:13; Daniel 3:1-18; Hosea 11:2, 13:2-4; Micah 1:7, 5:12-13; Habakkuk 2:18-20.

Should We Pray to the Saints Themselves?

At this point, someone might suggest that even though it is wrong to pray to images, perhaps it would be all right to pray to the saints themselves, that they may serve as mediators between us and God. Jesus, however, said that no man could come to the father except by Him (John 14:6), and 1 Timothy is even more specific: *And the truth is this: God is one. One also is the mediator between God and men, the man Christ Jesus, who gave Himself as a ransom for all.* Christ is our mediator, because it is He who brings us into contact with God. He paid all that God required for our sins, so that we sinners may pray directly, "Our father..."

Another translation puts it this way, *for there is one God and one mediator between God and men, the man Christ Jesus, who gave himself as a ransom for all men.* Why would God tell us that Christ Jesus is the only mediator if it is a lie, and there are really many mediators?

A priest phoned to discuss this verse with me on a call-in TV program. Trying to point out a loop hole in this verse that would allow Catholics to pray to the saints, he stated: It is not that the saints can answer prayer directly, but they pray to Jesus who in turn prays to God the Father who answers the prayer. Knowing the Catholic doctrine, I asked, "Are the saints omniscient and omnipresent, so that they can understand thousands of prayers from all over the world in many different languages, all at the same time?" He, of course, had to answer, "No, only God is omniscient and omnipresent, the saints can't hear and understand all those prayers." Realizing the implication of what he had said, he tried to repair the damage by saying, "God the Father hears the prayers and tells the saints what it was that the people asked for!!!"

Remember, only God can be in all places at once to hear the thousands of prayers coming from all around the world at the same time. Can you think of a good reason not to pray to Him in the first place?

God loves us. He wants to be our friend and our Father. He asks us to pray directly to Him, to have communion with Him, to honor Him and to praise Him. He feels left out when we venerate someone or something else. The Bible tells us that He is jealous of our love, and helps us understand this by giving us the illustration of a husband who doesn't want his wife going out with other men. What are we saying to God when we turn our backs on Him and pray to a saint? It is a great offense to infer that He is not as kind, considerate, and compassionate as the saints are.

Let's examine an example which literally hundreds of Italians have used to show me why I should pray to the saints. They say, "If you wanted a job in a certain factory, and your uncle was the friend of the owner, you would not go directly to the factory owner yourself. You would ask your uncle to go to the owner for you". In this illustration, the uncle represents the saint, and the factory owner represents God. The illustration implies that the saint, represented by the uncle, knows and loves you, and wishes to help you, while God, who is represented by the factory owner, does not. The truth is that God knows and loves us, and asks us to come directly to Him in the name of Jesus Christ, the only mediator.

The Bible never infers that any saints, living or dead, sympathize with us more than God does, nor does it even once mention the possibility of anyone praying to or through them. It does, however, say of Christ, *For we do not have a high priest who is unable to sympathize with our weakness, but one who was tempted in every way that we are, yet never sinned. So let us confidently approach the throne of grace to receive mercy and favor and to find help in time of need.* (Hebrews 4:15-16, read also Ephesians 3:12). He knows, and he cares!

Christ Himself tells us to whom we should pray. Matthew 7:7-11, begins: *Ask, and you will receive...* It ends, *If you, with all your sins, know how to give your children what is good, how much more will your heavenly Father give good things to anyone who asks him!* John 15:16 adds that we should ask the Father in Jesus' name. *It was not you who chose me, it was I who chose you to go forth and bear fruit. Your fruit must endure, so that all you ask the Father in my name he will give you.* A study of the prayers in the Bible will show you that all were addressed to God the Father, and none to saints who had died.

Do Protestants Believe in the Saints?

What I have just said will lead some to state, "The Protestants don't believe in the saints! " Actually, we do believe in the saints! However, we believe what the Bible says about them, which is very different from Catholic tradition. We believe in them so much that we want to obey the commandments that God inspired them to write in the Bible. Among other things, they have told us that we are to pray to God and not to saints or images. In addition to trying to obey what the saints have written in the Bible, those saints who were really saints, serve as examples to us. The Bible calls all who are sanctified through faith in the Lord Jesus Christ, "saints", a word which in the New Testament is used to refer to believers as a group, not to distinguish one person as being more saintly than another because he did miracles or lived a purer life.

In the Bible the term "saints" is used to describe people who were still living. Paul's writings in the Bible use the word a great deal. Let's examine how he uses it. *...to all the saints who are at Ephesus...* (Ephesians 1:1). (I have quoted this from the older Roman Catholic Douay version which agrees with almost all other translations. The new Catholic translation which I have been using, though generally quite accurate, translates this word in other ways.)

See also Ephesians 1:15,18; 2:19; 3:8,18; 4:12; 5:3, and 6:18; Romans 1:7; Acts 9:13,32; 26:10. One cannot help but be struck by the fact that the word "saint" was consistently used in the plural to refer to the groups of normal Christians.

The believers from the church in Corinth were saints (1 Corinthians 1:2, 6:11, 14:34). Yet they still had some extremely grave defects and sins and Paul could not speak to them as to spiritual Christians, but as carnal (1 Corinthians 1:11, 3:1, 6:5-8, 11:22).

Why Don't Protestants Pray to the Saints?

In addition to the clear statement, *God is one. One also is the mediator between God and men...,* there are other reasons why we do not pray to the saints:

• God gives us no example in the Bible of anyone who ever prayed to the saints or venerated them, nor does He give us any indication that He wants us to do this.

• The Scripture further says: *You shall do homage to the Lord your God; Him alone shall you adore* (Luke 4:8).

• In the Bible, we find illustrations of both men and angels refusing to permit people to bow before them, and in fact teaching that this should not be done. *As Peter entered, Cornelius went to meet him, dropped to his knees before him and bowed low. Peter said as he helped him to his feet, "Get up! I am only a man myself."* Acts 10:25-26, see also Acts 14:13-15, and Revelations 22:8-9).

• The apostle Paul, one of the "saints", explained to the Philippians that he could only be of help to them alive. (Philippians 1:23-26).

To answer the argument that saints do answer prayer with miracles, we must respond with the reminder that spiritual manifestations (including miracles) can come from two different places: God, or the devil and his demons. God's command is that we must not make images. When miracles seem to be done by the saints, and convince more people to take part in the idolatrous practice of praying to someone other than God, these miracles can hardly be from God.

In addition, there are a number of saints who have been deposed by the Catholic church because historic studies have shown that they never existed. Saint Philomena, for example, was supposed to have miraculously healed Pope Pious the Tenth. However, more recently this saint was debunked by another pope and his investigating commission as pure fable. In spite of the fact that the official position of the church now is that no such person ever existed, those who are faithful to her image claim that it continues to perform miracles.

You, too, can become a saint if you will come through faith in Jesus Christ who said, *I am the way, and the truth, and the life; no one comes to the Father but through me.* (John 14:6). It is not an official statement by the church that makes one a saint, neither is it earned by living a sinless life or by doing miracles. God makes saints out of sinners: *...we have been sanctified through the offering of the body of Jesus Christ once for all* (Hebrews 10:10, read also Acts 26:18). Trust in the Lord Jesus Christ to take away your sins, and you too will become one of the saints.

5

Why Are Evangelical Pastors Permitted To Marry?

The Bible makes it clear both in the Old Testament and the New, that marriage is not prohibited to those who would like to please God, even to those who want to serve Him full time. The New Testament makes this clear when it sets out the requirements for church officers. *A bishop must be irreproachable, married only once... He must be a good manager of his own household, keeping his children under control* (Timothy 3:2-4). This is the same rule that is given for the deacons, *Deacons may be married but once, and must be good managers of their children and their households* (3:12). The priests of the Old Testament were also free to marry and were usually married, just as were the church leaders of the New Testament.

In addition, while severely condemning all sexual relations between people who are not married to each other, God explains that sexual contact between people who are married is not sin. Rather, He commands each person in the marriage union to give himself to the other. *But to avoid immorality, every man should have his own wife and every woman her own husband. The husband should fulfill his conjugal obligations toward his wife, the wife hers toward her husband. A wife does not belong to herself but to her husband; equally, a husband does not belong to himself but to his wife. Do not deprive one another, unless perhaps by mutual consent for a time to devote yourselves to prayer. Then return to one another...* (1 Corinthians 7:1-5). This passage makes it very clear that lack of desire at the moment, or even a feeling that sex is sin, is not sufficient reason for a married person to deprive his husband or wife. God wants married people to be satisfied at home, so as to be strengthened against temptation from without.

In Ephesians 5:22-23, God chose the relationship between husband and wife as an example of His relationship with the believers. He said, *Wives should be submissive to their husbands as if to the Lord because the husband is the head of his wife just as Christ is head of His body the church, as well as its Savior.* The passage goes on to command husbands to love their wives, and treat them tenderly, as nicely as they treat themselves. We are to be submissive to Christ, as the wife is to be submissive to her husband, and He cares for us in the way that he wants a husband to care for his wife. The use of this comparison shows that God approves of marriage.

It is true that an unmarried person is more free to do God's work, and the Bible states this clearly, but balances it with the teaching of 1 Corinthians 7:9, *but if they cannot exercise self-control, they should marry. It is better to marry than to be on fire.* So while the unmarried condition is the best way for some people to serve God, it is not the best for everyone. That is why God permits each one to marry or not, as seems best in his own case.

The Catholic church maintains that Peter was the first Bishop of Rome and the first Pope, yet he was clearly married as we see in Matthew 8:14 and 1 Corinthians 9:5. Since the Bible does not command celibacy for the church leaders, and the early church did not practice it, obviously it is not a commandment of God for all those who want to serve Him full time. It was imposed upon the Roman Catholic priests by certain synods (Elvira, Orange, Arles, Agde, Toledo) and by the Lateran Council of 1139, basically to eliminate nepotism in the Roman church which controls a great deal of property which some of the priests preferred to pass on to their children.

This condition does not exist in most Protestant churches, so there has been little need of this kind of regulation. In addition, many Protestant churches are too democratic in their organization to be able to impose a rule which has no Biblical basis. The Roman Church as an employer has the right to require celibacy of some of its employees; however, many priests are incapable of making it through life without having sexual relations. God considers these relations extremely sinful when practiced by those who are not married (1 Corinthians 6:9-10,18; Acts 15:28-29; Revelations 21:8). The poor priests who are not able to resist will not only be more severely condemned by God, but also scandalize many in their church, and bring other people into sin with them.

6

Do You Believe In Mary?

Yes! We do believe all that the Word of God tells us of Mary. The beliefs that we reject are those which men have come up with later without any Biblical basis. We believe that Mary was a virtuous woman, chosen by God to be the mother of Jesus Christ. Moreover, she was a virgin at His birth. On the other hand, we do not pray to Mary nor make images of her because the Bible teaches: *You shall do homage to the Lord your God; Him alone shall you adore* (Luke 4:8). The Bible consistently teaches that prayer should be directed to God the Father. When the disciples asked Jesus, "Teach us to pray," the first thing He said was "when you pray, say Our Father..." and then went on to teach the Lord's prayer. Jesus once asked another group of people, "Why do you call me Lord, Lord, and then not do what I say?" Since Jesus asks us to pray to the Father, let's do it!

Sometimes those who want us to pray to Mary say that since she was the mother of Jesus, He always granted her everything she asked of Him. You may judge for yourself whether or not this is true after reading the following passage from the Bible. *His mother and his brothers arrived, and as they stood outside they sent word to Him to come out. The crowd seated around Him told Him, "Your mother and your brothers and sisters are outside asking for you." He said in reply, "Who are my mother and my brothers? and gazing around Him at those seated in the circle He continued, "These are my mother and my brothers. Whoever does the will of God is brother and sister and mother to me"* (Mark 3:31-35).

In the Bible, there is no example of anyone ever trying to go to Jesus or God the Father through Mary. Instead we read, *God is one. One also is the mediator between God and men, the man Christ Jesus who gave Himself as a ransom for all* (1 Timothy 2:5-6). Jesus said, *I am the way, and the truth, and the life; no one comes to the Father but through me.* (John 14:6). Christ is the only mediator. He puts us directly in touch with God by taking away the sins that separated us, so that we can come to Him directly.

History informs us that prayers to Mary began around the end of the fourth century after Christ. Certainly if she had still been alive she would not have permitted this practice! As a pious woman, she would never have accepted prayer, as it should be directed to God alone.

In Italy, the very center of Roman Catholicism, people tend to pray to the various images of Mary. Furthermore, they commonly believe each individual image has particular abilities. A number are believed to possess the power to heal in an exceptional way. Others protect from the lava of Mt. Vesuvius. Others are thought to protect particular groups of people, such as fishermen. The churches with statues which are particularly revered promote this belief.

As a result, many people will drive for miles, passing hundreds of images of Mary to get to the one they think can help them the most. This is obviously idolatry and it is not this that I wish to discuss here as it has nothing to do with Mary who is one. Her powers do not change from statue to statue.

Rather, let us look at Mary, the mother of Jesus, a real woman like many of you who are reading this book. We believe that she was a fine woman, because God chose her for a very special task which would bring her to prominence and cause her to be held up as an example. There is, however, no reason to believe that she was conceived without sin, because after the birth of Christ we find her in the temple offering a sacrifice for her purification (Luke 2:22-24). This is the same action that all the Hebrew women took after childbirth (Leviticus 12). In addition, in her prayer of thanksgiving for being chosen to be the mother of Christ, Mary calls God *my Savior* (Luke 1:47). Had she been born without sin, she would not have needed either an offering for purification, or a savior.

The church of Rome teaches that Mary should be called the mother of God, an expression that is never used in the Bible. The reasoning is that she is the Mother of Jesus Christ, and He is God. While at first glance the reasoning sounds acceptable, if she were the mother of God, we would have to conclude that the creature was the mother of the creator: that is that Mary, who was born at a particular moment of history, was the mother of everything about God which has existed from all eternity (Genesis 1:1; John 1:1-3, 14). The Bible does not teach this. Instead, it teaches that God, who has always existed, took on a human nature by means of the virgin birth. Thus Mary was the mother of Christ's human nature, but not of His divine nature which has existed from all eternity (John 8:57-58). To avoid causing confusion on this point, we prefer not to use the term mother of God.

While the Bible teaches that Mary was a virgin at Christ's birth, it gives us no reason to believe that she remained a virgin all of her lifetime. In fact, Mary was obedient to God who, when speaking of married people, said that the man shall leave his father and mother and cleave to his wife and that they two should become one flesh (Ephesians 5:31 and Matthew 19:6). Speaking specifically about Mary and Joseph, the Bible explains: *He had no relations with her at any time before she bore a son, whom he named Jesus* (Matthew 1:25). This passage obviously establishes the fact that Joseph had not had relations with Mary before the birth of Jesus, and other passages clearly declare that she was a virgin at His birth. Stating, *He had no relations with her at any time before she bore a son,* however, purposely excludes from the time in which they had no relations, the time after she had a son. Neither do any of the other passages which speak of Mary's virginity ever infer that she was to remain a virgin after Christ's birth. Rather, it is implied that after the birth of Christ, Mary and Joseph had normal husband-wife relations. To maintain that Mary remained a virgin all of her life infers that she did not obey God's will for married women, and this does not really honor her.

Who Were the Brothers of Jesus?

In addition to inferring that Mary did not remain a virgin forever, the Bible speaks of Christ's brothers a number of times as well. In the gospel of Matthew, we read, *Isn't Mary known to be His mother and James, Simon, and Judas His brothers? Aren't His sisters our neighbors?* (Matthew 13:55-56). After the birth of Christ, almost every time that the Bible speaks of Mary she is with Christ's brothers. As far as we can tell, they all lived together as a normal family (see Matthew 12:46, 13:55-56; Mark 3:31, 6:3; Luke 8:19; John 2:12). Some Catholics maintain that the brothers of Christ were in reality cousins. Many older translations of the Catholic Bible translated the word "brothers" as "cousins" with no textual basis, and only in the case of the brothers of Jesus Christ. Everyone else's brothers were translated as brothers. The dishonesty of this kind of translation was so apparent that almost all recent Catholic translations use the word "brother".

Some Catholics say, "Yes, they were brothers, but only in the spiritual sense and not the physical." This interpretation is also in error because until after the resurrection, Christ's brothers did not believe in Him. John 7:5 puts it very clearly, *For neither did His brethren believe in Him* (The Roman Catholic Douay version, in agreement with virtually all others). If His brothers did not believe in Him, they were not "brothers" in the spiritual sense. The translators of the New American Bible evidently recognized the problem that this poses to the Roman teaching that Mary remained a virgin even after the birth of Christ. They have slightly weakened the statement in this translation as follows: *As a matter of fact, not even His brothers had much confidence in Him* (John 7:5). Several passages of the Bible actually distinguish between Christ's spiritual brothers and His physical brothers. One example of this is John 2:12. *After this He went down to Capernaum, along with His mother and brothers and His disciples...* (See also Matthew 12:46-50; Mark 3:31-35, 6:1-3; Luke 8:19-22). Passages like this make it clear that the Bible distinguishes between Christ's brothers and His disciples.

On the mistaken foundation of the perpetual virginity of Mary, philosophers down through the centuries have built a tower of fables; ideas that have no roots in the Bible or in other literature of the period in which Mary lived. Jesus Christ did not encourage the excessive glorification of Mary that is so common now. We read, *While He was saying this a woman from the crowd called out, "Blest is the womb that bore you and the breasts that nursed you!" "Rather," He replied, "Blest are they who hear the word of God and keep it,"* (Luke 11:27-28; See also Matthew 12:46-50; Mark 3:31-35).

Giving Mary the glory that should be given to God is not the right way to honor her. If I were to honor you by calling you "her majesty, the queen of England," or by saying that I think it is wonderful the way you bravely faced the perils of the ocean to discover America, would you feel honored? Probably you would think that I was either awfully ignorant, or else making fun of you. You would prefer it if I said something nice about what you really were or had done.

Another way that we can honor Mary is by doing that which would have pleased her. The Bible records only one commandment that Mary gave. It was given at the marriage in Cana, in Galilee: *Do whatever He tells you* (John 2:5). She was telling the waiters at the marriage dinner to obey whatever Christ told them. Since her commandment was given in a particular situation to specific people, we can avoid keeping it if we wish. Nevertheless, in our hearts, we know that Mary would be more pleased if we obey Christ than if we fail to, and then say that we are honoring her. So let's honor Mary in a way that does not go against any Scriptural teaching, a way that both she and God would approve of. Let's follow her command to do what Christ said.

7

Is There A Purgatory?

The Bible never speaks of a place where one can go to be purified of his sin. Rather, it always speaks of a Person to whom we can go to be purified: Jesus Christ. God tells us that those who refuse to trust Christ to cleanse them from their sins are condemned: *Whoever believes in Him avoids condemnation, but whoever does not believe is already condemned for not believing in the name of God's only Son* (John 3:18). There are only two choices: *Whoever believes in the Son has life eternal. Whoever disobeys the Son will not see life, but must endure the wrath of God* (John 3:36; See also Revelation 20:15; Luke 16:19-31, especially verse 26). Anyone who accepts Christ is completely saved: *There is no condemnation now for those who are in Christ Jesus* (Romans 8:1). Saying that there is no condemnation, certainly eliminates the flames of purgatory.

Another passage which clearly excludes the idea of purgatory is, *...their sins and transgressions I will remember no more* (Hebrews 10:17). If, as the Bible says, God no longer remembers the sins of those who are in Christ, He does not punish them for these sins. To do so would be saying that Christ had not made full payment for them and that God the Father still remembered them. (See also Romans 5:8-11; Hebrews 10:14-18; Psalm 103:12).

Anyone who does not believe that Christ has completely saved him, has not completely trusted Christ to save him. That is, he does not believe that Christ's sacrifice has paid for all of his sins, and thinks he must pay for some of them himself. However, we are saved when we stop trusting what we can do, and start trusting Christ to save us.

The idea that Christ's sacrifice is not sufficient to cleanse us from all of our sins would condemn a great sinner such as the thief who was crucified with Jesus to suffer a long time in purgatory if not for all eternity in hell! Instead, there was nothing left over that Christ's death on the Cross did not cover. When the thief placed his trust in Christ, Jesus said to him, *I assure you: this day you will be with me in paradise* (Luke 23:43).

If purgatory existed, and the mass helped people to get out, the rich would have a tremendous advantage by being able to pay for masses to shorten their suffering. The poor instead, would be left to the mercy of the occasional priest who might say an unpaid mass for them. One ex-priest wrote, "If we really believed that the mass would save people from the flames of purgatory, would we make them pay for it? I would even save a dog if I saw one in a fire, and I would never even think of asking to be paid!"

Purgatory was evidently a pagan idea. Virgil, the pagan Latin poet who lived 70 – 19 B.C. divided the departed souls into three different places in his writings: One for the good, one for the damned, and a third where the less bad could pay for their sins. Since the idea of purgatory existed outside of the church before it came into the church, it is probable that it was brought in by contact with pagans like Virgil. There was a great influx of non-Biblical ideas into the church around 300 A.D. when the Roman Emperor Constantine took many unsaved people in as members of the church.

In any event, there is no mention of purgatory in the Bible. Some would try, however, to make the idea sound somewhat Biblical by referring to 2 Maccabees 12:41-45, a passage in one of the apocryphal books written between the times of the Old and New Testaments. These books were never accepted as part of the Hebrew Old Testament, nor quoted in the New Testament, but they are included in the Catholic Bible, though usually with an explanation that they are of a less inspired category. Apart from this passage in 2 Maccabees, the apocrypha is little used by the Catholic church to support a doctrinal position.

It is important to notice that this passage does not speak of purgatory at all, but actually condemns idolatry, particularly the practice of wearing little images on a necklace or such. Hebrew soldiers were found wearing this sort of thing after a battle, and their buddies, on making this discovery, realized that they had died in the sin of idolatry. They then counseled prayer for their souls. The Roman Catholic position is that prayer for them would have been unnecessary if they were in heaven and useless if they were in hell, so there must be another place. The logic seems good, but the result contradicts the clear teaching of the inspired Scripture. Contradicting inspired Scripture

with a philosophical response based on an apparent infer-
ence from the Apocrypha is a very weak argument indeed.
The very word "Apocrypha," which comes from the Greek
word for hidden, has come to mean "false," or "of doubtful
authorship."

8

On Whom Is The Church Founded?

The Apostle Peter himself explained in the Bible on whom the church was founded. He said that Jesus was the cornerstone: *This Jesus is the stone rejected by you the builders which has become the cornerstone. There is no salvation in anyone else, for there is no other name in the whole world given to men by which we are to be saved* (Acts 4:11-12).

To have a Biblical basis for the papacy, the Roman Catholic church neglects the numerous passages such as the one above which clearly teach that Christ is the head and foundation of the church, and quotes a short part of a passage from the Gospel of Matthew. They neglect to realize that even if the church was founded on Peter, there is nothing in this passage to infer that his status was passed on to the popes. I quote that passage here, with a few verses which precede it, and will add to our understanding.

They replied, "some say John the Baptizer, others Elijah, still others Jeremiah or one of the prophets." "And you, who do you say that I am?"

"You are the Messiah," Simon Peter answered, "the Son of the living God!"

Jesus replied, "Blest are you, Simon son of Jonah! No mere man has revealed this to you, but my heavenly Father. I for my part declare to you, you are "Rock," and on this rock I will build my church, and the jaws of death shall not prevail against it (Matthew 16:14-18). In Greek, the original language of the New Testament, Christ calls Peter "Rock" (masculine gender) then says "on this rock" (feminine gender) I will build my church. What is the rock on which the church is built? The usual Catholic interpretation is Peter, but the difference in gender makes this questionable. Then, just five verses ahead, Jesus reproves Peter with such severity that He calls him Satan. In the context itself then, it is equally possible that the "rock" upon which the church is founded is found in the statement that Peter made, *You are the Messiah, the Son of the living God.*

If we will let the passages in other parts of the Bible that refer to the same subject help us decide who it is that the church is founded upon, we find that it is Christ. *No one can lay a foundation other than the one that has been laid, namely Jesus Christ* (1 Corinthians 3:11).

Peter certainly should have understood whether the church was founded on himself or on Christ, and he wrote that it was on Jesus Christ: *For Scripture has it: "See, I am laying a cornerstone in Zion, an approved stone, and precious. He who puts his faith in it shall not be shaken." The stone is of value for you who have faith. For those without faith, it is rather, "A stone which the builders rejected that became a cornerstone." It is likewise "an obstacle and stumbling stone." Those who stumble and fall are the dis-*

believers in God's word; it belongs to their destiny to do so (1 Peter 2:6-8). Peter understood Christ to be the cornerstone, the foundation of the church, and was obviously referring to Him in this passage.

Christ Himself said, *Are you not familiar with this passage of Scripture: The stone rejected by the builders has become the keystone of the structure* (Mark 12:10). The Jews understood that in saying this, Jesus was claiming to be their Messiah, and since they did not want Him to be their head they immediately tried to kill Him, stumbling on the stone, as the Scriptures had predicted. Later they succeeded, but He rose from the dead and became the stone upon which the church was founded. Will you accept Christ as the foundation and director of your life?

Returning then, to Matthew 16:14-18, with this background from the Scriptures, it seems clear that *The rock* to which Jesus referred was not Peter himself, but his confession: *You are the messiah, the Son of the living God.*

Even if this were not true, and Peter were the rock upon which the church was founded, there is still no Biblical reason to think that Peter's authority was passed on to others, and that the popes are his successors. Neither is there reason to believe that this idea was accepted by the early church. In fact the idea of a "pope" developed a little bit at a time and it was only in 1870 that the infallibility of the pope became a dogma. Even then there was a strong opposition to the idea from within the Roman Catholic church itself. There is just no real foundation to the idea that one man, other than Jesus Christ Himself, has the authority over us that the Pope claims to have, although there are good reasons why he may want us to believe it.

It is also rather confusing that the Pope ties his claim to authority, infallibility, and the right to have others bow down to him, to his being the successor to Peter. Peter certainly never claimed these things. Just the opposite! When one tried to bow before him he said, *Get up! I am only a man myself* (Acts 10:26).

In addition, Paul found it necessary to rebuke Peter very severely, not because he was infallible, but because he was wrong. He wrote, *When Cephas (Peter) came to Antioch I directly withstood him, because he was clearly in the wrong* (Gal. 2:11). Nor was this the first big mistake that Peter made. We all remember how Peter denied Christ three times at the very moment of our Lord's trial and condemnation. I don't want to take away anything from this great apostle, but it is not logical to claim that the pope's infallibility was handed down to him from a man who made mistakes and his authority over the church came from a man who refused to let people bow down to him.

Since the true church is founded on Jesus Christ, we should find a church that does not preach another salvation based on works and sacraments, but one which has as its base the Holy Bible, and the one *name in the whole world given to men by which we are to be saved.* Since virtually everything that can be known about Christ is found in the Bible, don't go to a church which has some other authority, whether it be the pope, the Book of Mormon, the Watch Tower, or even its own pastor's alleged communications with God. If you can be comfortable in a church without taking your Bible, there is probably something wrong.

9

To Whom Should We Confess?

You will remember that when the disciples asked Jesus Christ to teach them to pray, He started His explanation, *This is how you are to pray: "Our Father in heaven..."* (Matthew. 6:9-14). Jesus was teaching them and through them teaching us, that our prayers should be directed to God the Father. Farther along in this prayer to our Father, Jesus continued, ...*and forgive us the wrong we have done as we forgive those who wrong us* (Matthew 6:12). Our Lord Jesus Christ Himself in this most famous of all prayers taught us to pray to God the Father, and to ask forgiveness of Him. Luke puts it this way, *Forgive us our sins for we too forgive all who do us wrong* (Luke 11:4). We confess our sins directly to God the Father, not because as Protestants we want to be different, but because that is the way Jesus taught His disciples to pray.

This was the normal way in which Christians confessed their sins in the first centuries of the church. Confession to the priest became official Catholic doctrine in 1225 A.D. Priests had started hearing confessions some time before this, but they prayed to God for the person rather than claiming to remit the sins themselves, as they do now.

In order to uphold the practice of confession being made to them, some priests refer to the passage in John; *As the Father has sent me, so I send you. Then He breathed on them and said: "Receive the Holy Spirit. If you forgive men's sins, they are forgiven them; if you hold them bound, they are held bound"* (John 20:21-23). The first thing we must notice is that these words were not spoken only to the apostles or to any other special class, but to all Christ's followers who were together at that time. Remitting sins is therefore not a privilege of the clergy, but extended to all believers.

In addition, we must ask, how did those who were present and heard Christ's words interpret them? What did they do to obey? They evidently understood that sins are forgiven when people trust in Christ as savior, because they went out and preached the good news that by trusting in Christ Jesus we have the forgiveness of sin (Acts 2:37-38, 10:43). They did not go out and listen to confessions, nor tell anyone that they themselves were remitting sins. The book of Acts is the history of what the early Christians did, and how God worked through them to spread the Gospel in that time. If you are still in doubt, a careful study of this book will convince you.

The episode in John 20, from which we have examined verses 21-23 is also found in Luke 24:36-48 with the addition of a very important detail: *He said to them: Thus it is written that the Messiah must suffer and rise from the dead on the third day. In His name, penance and the remission of sins is to be preached to all the nations, beginning at Jerusalem. You are witnesses of this* (24:26-

48). Christ was speaking about preaching repentance ("penance" is a poor translation) and the remission of sins and not of confessing our sins to man. By asking, "What did those who heard him do?" and studying out the answer in the Bible, we can easily see what our Lord meant: Witnessing to Christ, and proclaiming his salvation is what they understood that Christ was telling them to do, and that is what they did. The confessionals came hundreds of years later.

You may ask, "Do we need to confess our sins, or not?" Yes! Every Christian should confess his sins, but our confessions should not be made to man because only God has the power to forgive. The apostle John wrote, *But if we acknowledge our sins, he who is just can be trusted to forgive our sins and cleanse us from every wrong* (1 John 1:9). This Biblical exhortation to confess our sins to God is quite clear, but in case there should be any misunderstanding, almost all translations use "confess" where this one uses acknowledge. Also, as you read the preceding verses, you will see that *he who is just* is clearly referring to God.

We should confess our sins to God, trusting Him to forgive us on the basis of Christ's blood which was shed for our sins. As we trust Him, we will find that as His word says, *He who is just can be trusted to forgive our sins and cleanse us from every wrong.*

If we have sinned against some person, the Bible teaches us to ask that person's forgiveness also. Therefore if I have sinned against a priest, I should confess that sin to him as well as to God. There are also times that we need to talk to someone else about what we have done. The idea however, of confessing to a priest in place of confessing to God, is never found in the Scriptures.

Praying directly to your Father in Heaven, confess to Him all the sins that you can remember having committed, and trust that Christ paid for every one of them. Then in the future, when you fall into some sin, you should immediately confess that sin to God as well.

Conclusion

Dear friend, we have explained the clear teaching of the Bible. God invites you to accept His salvation now. It would be folly to continue in a system that has left God's word and substituted that of men. There is no real salvation in the Roman Catholic Church.

Walking through the famous church of Saint Peter in Rome as a tourist one day, I kept close to a group of school children so that I could hear the priest who was guiding them explain the interesting features of the building. Down in the basement, an interesting thing happened when we came to the tomb of Pope John the twenty third, who at that time was the last pope to die. The priest asked the children to kneel and pray that the soul of this great pope might soon be liberated from purgatory.

For all practical purposes, burning in purgatory until you have sufficiently paid for your own sins is the best that the Roman system of salvation by works has to offer. Why turn your back on the sure and only salvation that God offers you through Jesus Christ in order to remain in a system in which not even the greatest of the popes can be assured of finding salvation? Jesus said, *I am the way, and the truth, and the life; no one comes to the Father but through me* (John 14:6).

God loves you and in Jesus Christ has completely provided for your entrance into heaven. He invites you to put your faith in Christ, believing that He saves. Why not just bow your head in prayer, and make the decision right now to trust Christ to save you and to follow Him as your Lord. It is the only way to have peace with God and the salvation of your soul. ...*justified by faith, we are at peace with God through our Lord Jesus Christ* (Romans 5:1).